Mother Earth
Father Sky

All is beautiful,
All is beautiful,
All is beautiful, indeed.
Now the Mother Earth
And the Father Sky,
    Meeting, joining one another
    Helpmates ever, they.
    All is beautiful,
    All is beautiful,
    All is beautiful, indeed.

Navajo

Mother Earth
Father Sky

Pueblo and Navajo Indians of the Southwest
by Marcia Keegan

Clear Light Publishers   New Mexico

I want to thank all my friends for their support and help through the years, especially my longtime Pueblo and Navajo friends, the Pablita Velarde family, Julia Roybal, Leon & Reyne Roybal, Gary Roybal, Bernice Roybal, Leandra & Josephine Bernal, Phillip Bernal, the late Reyecita Bernal, Peter McDonald, Sam Day III, Shirley Lowe, the Thomas Banyacya family, the Lucy Martinez family, Rosemarie Cordova, Agnes Dill, August Shattuck, Veronica Chapman, Ramalda Shattuck, Isadora Sarracino. My appreciation for making this book possible also goes to Letta & Keith Wofford, Howard Bryan, K.D. & Dan Fullerton, Ruth N. Wilcox, Sophie McConnell, Eleanor Caponigro, Bobbi Burger, Bud Wescott, and Valerie Shepherd.

I also want to thank my husband, Harmon Houghton and especially Richard L. Grossman who first published this book.

Revised edition published by Clear Light Publishers
Published in 1974 by Grossman Publishers
ISBN 940666—05—7
Library of Congress Catalogue Card Number: 73—7091
Page 112 constitutes a continuation of this copyright page.

*The text of this book was set in Souvenir Light & Medium
by Emery Printing and University Graphics
The book was printed and bound in Hong Kong
by Book Art Inc, Toronto, Canada
Conceptual design by Bo Zaunders and Eleanor Caponigro
Cover design by Eleanor Caponigro
Title-page photograph: Dancer at Taos Pueblo
Cover photograph: Willie Cly, Navajo Sheep Herder*

To My Friends, with love

Beauty and harmony are the heart of the Indian way of life on the southwestern deserts.

The sun and the sky represents the father figure. Sunlight and rain, descending from the sky, are viewed as life-giving substances that promote fertility within the body of the mother earth.

But this beauty and harmony are in danger of being destroyed. This book attempts to show the relationship with nature that Pueblo and Navajo Indians now enjoy but which their children may loose if their mystic landscape becomes victim to continued pollution and scarring.

Through the photographs I have tried to recreate the sense of wonder and harmony with nature which is the integral part of Indian life. The chants that are included are expressions of the Indian spirit evoked by the natural beauty that surrounds them.

The Pueblo and Navajo Indians have much to teach us about how to live with nature, not just in practical terms based on their long successful existence in a harsh land, but in spiritual terms that are a foundation for their way of life. These teachings are most potently expressed in the rituals and gestures of daily traditional life which I have sought to portray in these photographs, and in the chants that accompany those rituals and express their higher meaning.

Marcia Keegan

Mother Earth
Father Sky

It is lovely indeed, it is lovely indeed.
I, I am the spirit within the earth . . .
The feet of the earth are my feet . . .
The legs of the earth are my legs . . .
The bodily strength of the earth is my bodily strength . . .
The thoughts of the earth are my thoughts . . .
The voice of the earth is my voice . . .
The feather of the earth is my feather . . .
All that belongs to the earth belongs to me . . .
All that surrounds the earth surrounds me . . .
I, I am the sacred words of the earth . . .
It is lovely indeed, it is lovely indeed.

Navajo

Monument Valley, Navajoland

There in the west
    is the home of the raingods,
There in the west
    is their water pool,
In the middle of the water pool
    is the spruce tree
    that they use as a ladder,
Up from the water the raingods
    draw the crops which give us life,
East from there, on the place
    where we dance, they lay the crops,
Then up from that place the people
    receive crops and life.

                      Acoma

Water pool in Monument Valley

Canyon de Chelly

Running water, running water, herein resounding,
As on the clouds I am carried to the sky,
Running water, running water, herein roaring,
As on the clouds I am carried to the sky.

Zuñi

Now the Mother Earth
And the Father Sky,
Meeting, joining one another,
Helpmates ever, they.
    All is beautiful,
    All is beautiful,
    All is beautiful, indeed.

Navajo

El Capitan

In a holy place with a god I walk,
In a holy place with a god I walk,
On a chief of mountains with a god I walk,
In old age wandering with a god I walk,
On a trail of beauty with a god I walk.

Navajo

Desert mirage

Southwest rainbow

The rainbow raised up with me.
Through the middle of broad fields,
The rainbow returned with me.
To where my house is visible,
The rainbow returned with me.

Navajo

Taos Pueblo

Yonder comes the dawn,
The universe grows green,
The road to the underworld
Is open! Yet now we live
Upward going, upward going!

Tewa

Plastering adobe home, Taos Pueblo

Do not forget your house.
Here in your own house
You will go about happily.
Always talking together kindly
We shall pass our days.

Zuñi

Adobe mantel at Taos Pueblo

Nambe dancers leaving kiva

In the chief's kiva
They, the fathers,
They and Muyingwa
Plant the double ear-corn.
Plant the perfect double corn-ear.
So the fields shall shine
With tassels white of perfect corn-ears.

Hopi

Rain Kachina

Nambe Deer Dancers

The deer, the deer, here he went,
Here are his tracks over mother earth, mother earth;
Tramping, tramping through the deep forest
with none to disturb him from above or below.

Cochiti

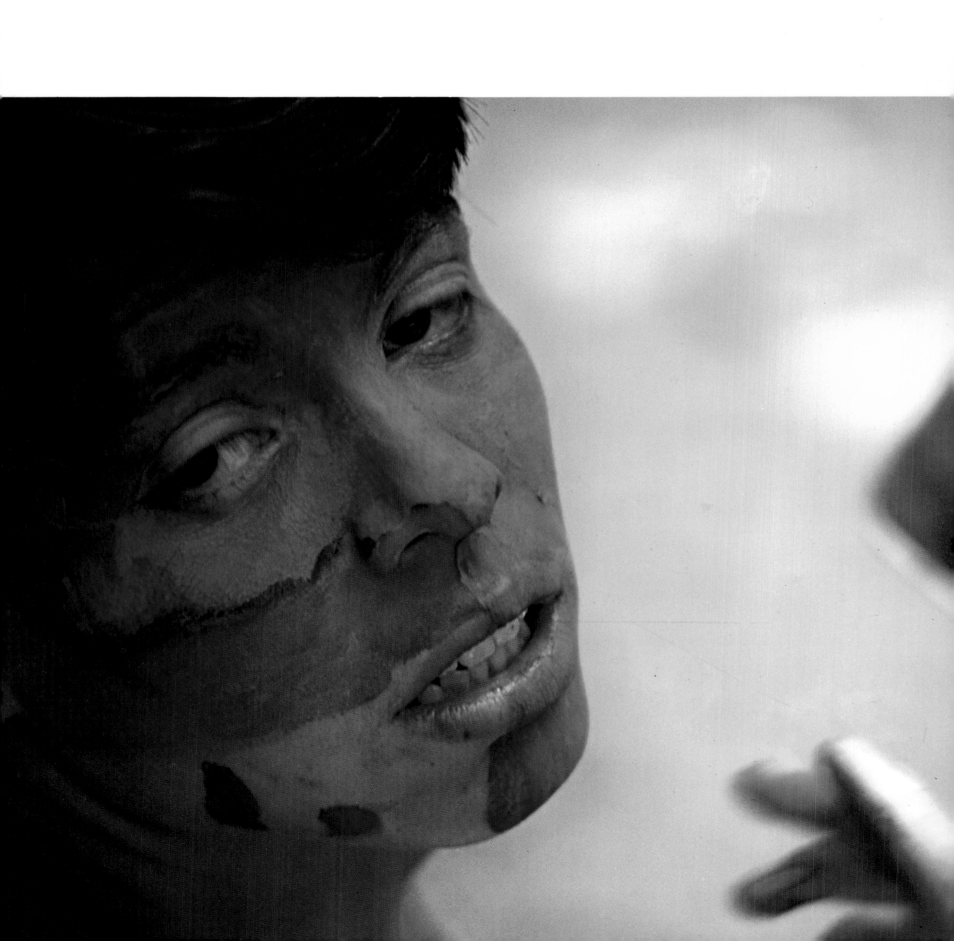

Round Dance at Taos Pueblo

The Plumes of the warriors
placed duly in lines,
To the Eastward before them;
The warriors made ready for travel.

Cochiti

Preparing for a Nambe dance

May you grow old:
May your roads be fulfilled;
May you be blessed with life;
To where the life-giving road
of your sun father comes out,
May your roads reach
May your roads all be fulfilled.

Zuñi

Earth Magician makes the mountains.
  Heed what he has to say!
He it is that makes the mesas.
  Heed what he has to say!

Tewa

Monabe, Hopi

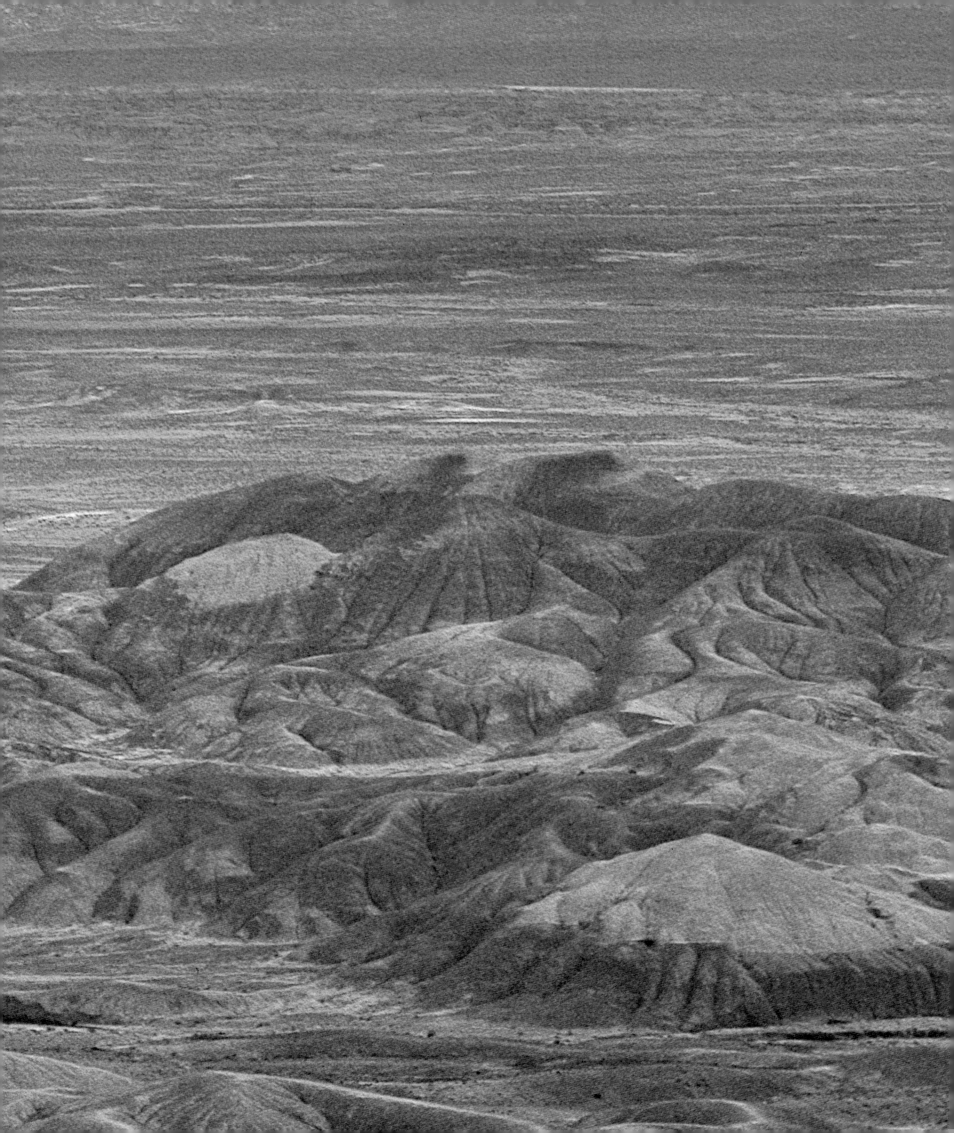

The Earth is looking at me;
she is looking up at me
I am looking down on her
I am happy, she is looking at me
I am happy, I am looking at her.

The Sun is looking at me;
he is looking down on me
I am looking up at him
I am happy, he is looking at me
I am happy, I am looking at him.

Navajo

Navajo child, Lauren Cly, in Monument Valley

Oh our Mother the Earth, Oh our Father the Sky,
Your children are we, and with tired backs
We bring you the gifts that you love.
Then weave for us a garment of brightness;

May the warp be the white light of morning,
May the weft be the red light of evening,
May the fringes be the falling rain,
May the border be the standing rainbow.

Thus weave for us a garment of brightness
That we may walk fittingly where birds sing,
That we may walk fittingly where grass is green,
Oh our Mother the Earth, Oh our Father the Sky.

Tewa

Navajo weaver at home

Navajo "Yei" rug on loom

Now I cannot say what they will make of me.
I may take the form of a cloud;
I wish I could be a cloud.
I take the chance of whatever is offered to me.
When a cloud comes this way, you will say,
"That is he!"
When I get to the place of spirits,
I will hear everything you ask.
You must always remember me.

Santo Domingo

Mystery Valley in Navajoland

Navajo rider

In the house of long life, there I wander.
In the house of happiness, there I wander.
Beauty before me, with it I wander.
Beauty behind me, with it I wander.
Beauty below me, with it I wander.
Beauty above me, with it I wander.
Beauty all around me, with it I wander.
In old age traveling, with it I wander.
On the beautiful trail I am, with it I wander.

Navajo

Acoma Pueblo home

Let us go to the Indian village, said all the rain gods,
so that the people of the village will be happy again.

Zuñi

Far as man can see,
Comes the rain,
Comes the rain with me.

From the Rain-Mount,
Rain-Mount far away,
Comes the rain,
Comes the rain with me.

Navajo

Standing rain

Let me see, if this be real,
Let me see, if this be real,
This life I am living?
Ye who possess the skies,
Let me see if this be real,
This life I am living.

Tewa

Juan José Martinez of Picuris

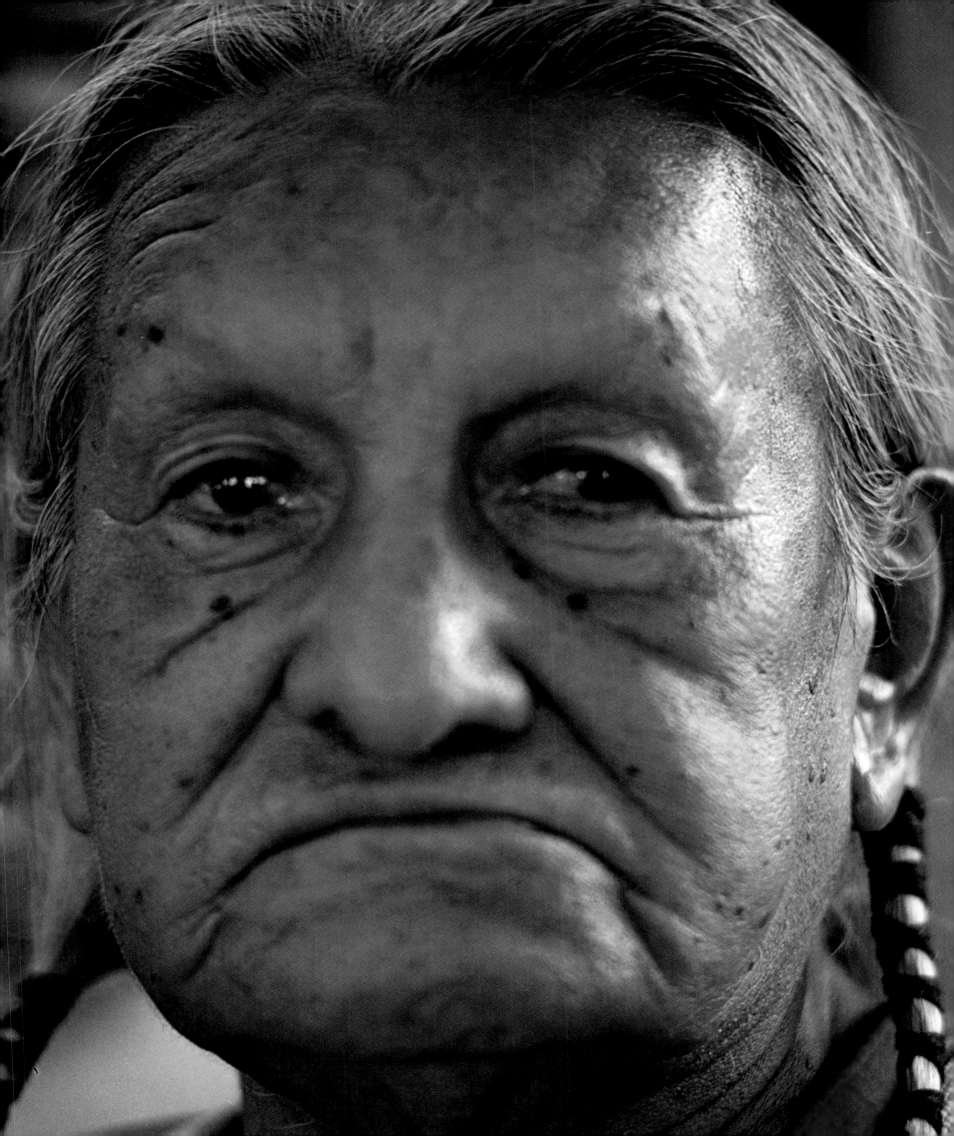

The earth has been laid down,
The earth has been laid down,
The earth has been laid down,
It has been made.

The Earth Spirit has been laid down,
It has been laid down,
The earth has been laid down,
It has been made.

Navajo

Winter in Monument Valley

Acoma Pueblo

Early this morning
the coming of the sun,

For what purpose is it coming?

Perhaps for sons and daughters
of the people it is coming.

Yonder in the west,
People, what do you think?
What do you say?
Shall we sit and sing?

Isleta

Hopi village of Hotevilla

Food offerings, Acoma Cemetery

Eat the food that now we bring you
and remember us no more.
Give us ample food, and now
no longer we remember you.

Tewa

Acoma Pueblo cemetery

Where my kindred dwell,
     There I wander.
The Red Rock House,
     There I wander.
In the house of long life,
     There I wander.
In the house of happiness,
     There I wander.
In old age traveling,
     With it I wander.
On the beautiful trail I am,
     With it I wander.

Navajo

White House Ruin, Canyon de Chelly

The ancients make their presence delightful.

Navajo

Anasazi petroglyphs, Monument Valley

The Holy Wind blows through his mane
His mane is made of rainbows

My horse's ears are made of round corn
My horse's eyes are made of stars
My horse's head is made of mixed waters
My horse's teeth are made of white shell

The long rainbow is in his mouth for a bridle
With it I guide him

When my horse neighs
Different-colored horses follow
When my horse neighs
Different-colored sheep follow

I am wealthy from my horse

Before me peaceful
Behind me peaceful
Under me peaceful
Over me peaceful
Around me peaceful
Peaceful voice when he neighs
I am everlasting and peaceful
I stand for my horse.

Navajo

Navajo sheep herder

Hopi corn field at Moenkopi

My great corn plants
Among them I walk
I speak to them
They hold out their hands to me.

Navajo

They shall dance for the increase
and strength of the corn-seed,
of each grain, making many,
Each grain that ye nourish
with new soil and water.

Zuñi

Ada Mirabal, Nambe Pueblo corn dancer Corn Dancer

Blue Corn with her grandchild, San Ildefonso Pueblo

Taos elder

May it be delightful, my fire;
May it be delightful for my children;
May all be well;
May it be delightful with my food and theirs;
May all my possessions be well, and may they be made
        to increase.

Navajo

May we be the ones whom your
thoughts will embrace,
For this, on this day
To our sun father,
We offer prayer meal.
To this end:
May you help us all to finish our
roads.

Zuñi

Corn Dance at San Ildefonso Pueblo

All the white-cloud eagles
Lift me up with your wings
Take me to the entrance to the earth

All you eagles
Lift me up with your wings
Lift me high over the world
Let no one see where you are taking me

Far to the southwest
Where our fathers and mothers have gone
Take me there with your wings
Place me there with your wings.

Santo Domingo

Laguna Pueblo Eagle Dancers

My words are tied in one
With the great mountains,
With the great rocks,
With the great trees,
In one with my body
And my heart.

Do you all help me
With supernatural power,
And you, Day!
And you, Night!
All of you see me,
One with this world!

Tewa

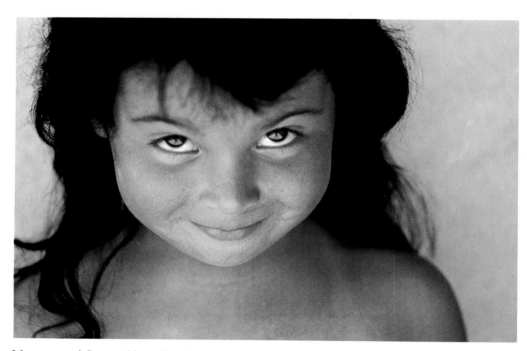

Margaret of Santa Clara Pueblo

Navajo weaver

In beauty may I walk.
Soft goods may I acquire.
Hard goods may I acquire.
Horses may I acquire.
Sheep may I acquire.

In old age wandering.
Trail beautiful.
Lively may I walk.

Navajo

Roylee Jackson, Navajo

Navajo hogan life

Victoria Big at her Navajo hogan

May my house be in harmony
From my head, may it be happy
To my feet, may it be happy
Where I lie, may it be happy
All above me, may it be happy
All around me, may it be happy.

Navajo

My dear, my dears, you yellow corn maidens,
As you rise up I see you
Then I sing for you.

Cochiti

San Juan woman winnowing corn

Taos Pueblo

Nambe dancer

House made of the dawn.
House made of evening light.
House made of the dark cloud.
House made of male rain.
House made of dark mist.
House made of female rain.
House made of pollen.
House made of grasshoppers.
Dark cloud is at the door.
The trail out of it is dark cloud.
The zigzag lightning stands high up on it.
Male deity!
Your offering I make.

Navajo

Richard and Lucy Martinez, San Ildefonso potters

In beauty may my male kindred dwell.
In beauty may my female kindred dwell.

Navajo

Santa Clara Buffalo Dancers

Far, far away from Buffalo Country
Hither now they come with their little ones,
Rapidly now they walk, rapidly they walk,
Even now they reach the Red Bird Cap.

O Buffalo Old Man, O Buffalo Old Woman!
Come hither rapidly with your little ones.

Tewa

Buffalo herd at Taos Pueblo

The people walk over me.
The old men all say to me, I am beautiful.

Navajo

Across Beautiful Valley

Navajo women, two generations

Dawn old women
Dawn matrons
Dawn maidens
Dawn girls . . .
Perhaps if we are lucky
Our Earth Mother
Will wrap herself in a fourfold robe
of white meal.

Zuñi

The curtain of daybreak it is hanging,
The Daylight Boy it is hanging,
From the land of day it is hanging;
Before him, as it dawns, it is hanging;
Behind him, as it dawns, it is hanging.
Before him, in beauty, it is hanging;
Behind him, in beauty, it is hanging;
From his voice, in beauty, it is hanging.

Navajo

Rock spires near Kayenta, Navajoland

Acoma Pueblo

The beginning of the world, I am thinking about it.
The beginning of the world, I am talking about it.

Navajo

Philip Bernal in Taos Pueblo

I wonder if the lone eyes are watching me?
I wonder if the lone eyes are watching me?
I wonder if the lone eyes are watching me?
I am he who has killed the monsters.
The lightning is before me.
All is beautiful behind me.

Navajo

Taos drummaker, Terecino Jiron

Mr. Espinoza, Taos Pueblo

The earth is rumbling
From the beating of our basket drums.
The earth is rumbling from the beating
    of our basket drums, everywhere humming
Earth is rumbling, everywhere raining.

Tewa

Tesuque drummers and singers

Laguna Pueblo

I am being instructed,
Talking God I am.

Navajo

Navajo sand painter

Clouds over Navajoland

Monument Valley

Wind now commences to sing;
wind now commences to sing.
The land stretches before me,
Before me stretches away.

Tewa

My children, my children,
The wind makes my head feathers sing—
The wind makes my head feathers sing—
My children, my children.

Tewa

Taos Pueblo dancers

Rainbow in Navajoland

Homeward now shall I journey,
Homeward upon the rainbow;
Homeward now shall I journey,
Lo, yonder the Holy Place.

Navajo

May it be delightful, my house;
From my head to my feet, may it be delightful;
Where I lie, all above me,
All around me, may it be delightful.

May it be delightful, my fire;
May it be delightful for my children;
May all be well;
May it be delightful with my food and theirs;
May all my possessions be well, and may they be made
to increase.

Navajo

Navajo hogan

The Bearer of the Moon
Arises with me,
Journeys with me,
Goes down with me,
Abides with me,
But sees me not.

Tewa

Taos Pueblo Mission Church

Hasten clouds
from the four world quarters;

Come snow in plenty, that
water may be abundant
when summer comes;

Come ice, cover the fields, that
the planting may yield abundance,

Let all hearts be glad.

San Ildefonso

Winter at Taos Pueblo   109

To this end, my fathers,
My children
May you be blessed with light.

Zuñi

Roybal family of San Ildefonso Pueblo

Northern N.M. sunset

PHOTOGRAPHIC SITES

ACOMA PUEBLO, (plates 44, 45, 52, 54, 55) a Pueblo Indian village situated atop a 357-foot high sandstone mesa about 60 miles west of Albuquerque, New Mexico. Believed to be at least 1,000 years old, the "Sky City," as it is sometimes called, lays claim to being the oldest continuously inhabited community in the United States.

CANYON DE CHELLY, (plates 14, 15, 32, 57) a spectacular canyon on the Navajo Reservation in northeastern Arizona, reaching depths of up to 1100 feet. The lower walls contain prehistoric cliff dwellings, dating from before 1300 A.D., occupied by ancestors of the Pueblo Indians before the Navajos arrived on the scene.

HOPI VILLAGES, (plates 26, 53, 62) a series of permanent Hopi Indian towns atop high mesas on the Hopi Indian Reservation in northern Arizona, a reservation surrounded on all sides by the Navajo Indian Reservation. Hopi Indians are famed for their ritualistic ceremonials and fine arts and crafts including their Kachina dolls, which are hand carved representations of masked dancers.

LAGUNA PUEBLO, (plates 69, 94) a Pueblo Indian village alongside Interstate 40, about 40 miles west of Albuquerque, New Mexico. Founded in about 1699, it is the youngest of New Mexico's 19 Indian pueblos, most of which date from about 1300 A.D.

MONUMENT VALLEY, (plates 10, 11, 13, 37, 38, 51, 58, 61, 65, 72, 73, 98) astride the Arizona-Utah border on the Navajo Reservation, a spectacular region of giant sandstone monoliths that rise high above the desert floor like huge monuments, used as the setting for many western movies.

NAMBE PUEBLO, (plates 27, 28, 30, 63) a small Pueblo Indian village about 20 miles north of Santa Fe, New Mexico.

NAVAJOLAND, (plates 39, 41, 43, 47, 74, 75, 85, 86, 87, 88, 96, 97, 102, 105) comprising the 14-million acre Navajo Reservation, largest Indian reservation in the United States, a semi-arid land covering an area about the size of the state of West Virginia. The major portion of the reservation is in northern Arizona, with borders extending east into northwestern New Mexico and north into southern Utah. Home of about 150,000 Navajo Indians, semi-nomadic in nature.

PICURIS PUEBLO, (plate 49) a small Pueblo Indian village in a mountain setting south of Taos in northeastern New Mexico.

SAN ILDEFONSO PUEBLO, (plates 67, 80, 81, 111) a Pueblo Indian village near the east bank of the Rio Grande about 20 miles north of Santa Fe, New Mexico. Home of a number of well-known Indian potters, including Blue Corn and the late Maria Martinez.

SAN JUAN PUEBLO, (plate 76) a Pueblo Indian village on the east bank of the Rio Grande about 30 miles north of Santa Fe, New Mexico. The first Spanish colonists in New Mexico settled briefly here in 1598 before moving south to found Santa Fe.

SANTA CLARA PUEBLO, (plate 21, 71, 79, 82) a Pueblo Indian village on the west bank of the Rio Grande about 25 miles north of Santa Fe, New Mexico.

SHIPROCK, (plate 19) a towering natural landmark of volcanic origin on the Navajo Reservation in northwestern New Mexico, rising about 1500 feet above the desert floor, so-called because of its resemblance to a giant sailing ship. The Navajos, who consider it a sacred place, call it "the winged rock," in reference to a legend that it once took wings and carried the Navajo people away from danger.

TAOS PUEBLO, (plates 23, 24, 25, 31, 78, 83, 91, 92, 93, 101, 107, 109) a Pueblo Indian village near the town of Taos, in northeastern New Mexico. The pueblo consists of two multi-storied apartment units, facing one another on opposite banks of a small stream. High above the pueblo, in the Sangre de Cristo Mountains, is Blue Lake, a sacred lake of the Taos Indians.

TESUQUE PUEBLO, (plate 95) a Pueblo Indian village about 10 miles north of Santa Fe, New Mexico.

ZUÑI PUEBLO, a large Pueblo Indian village about 40 miles south of Gallup, New Mexico, near the Arizona border. Zuñi Indians are famed for their elaborate dance ceremonials and hand-crafted silver and turquoise jewelry.

ACKNOWLEDGEMENTS

Dover Publications, Inc.: From *The Indian's Book* by Natalie Curtis. Reprinted through the permission of the publisher.

Liveright Publishing Corporation: From *American Indian Poetry* by George W. Cronyn. Permission of Liveright, Publishers, New York. Copyright © 1962 by George Cronyn.

William Morrow & Company, Inc. and Harold Ober Associates Inc.: From *The Magic World* by William Brandon. Copyright © 1971 by William Brandon. Reprinted by permission.

SOURCES OF CHANTS

Brandon, William. *The Magic World.* New York: William Morrow & Co., Inc., 1971. Chant on page 60.

Bunzel, Ruth. "Zuñi Ritual Poetry." *47th Annual Report of the Bureau of American Ethnology* (1929-1930). Washington, D.C.: U.S. Government Printing Office. Chants on pages 24, 33, 66, 111.

Cronyn, George. *American Indian Poetry.* New York: Liveright, 1962. Chants on pages 18, 35, 89, 100, 109.

Curtis, Natalie. *The Indian's Book.* New York: Dover Publications, Inc., 1968. Chants on pages 16, 27, 104.

Cushing, Frank H. "Outline of Zuñi Creation Myths." *13th Annual Report of the Bureau of American Ethnology* (1891-1892). Washington: G.P.O. Chants on pages 31, 62, 87.

Densmore, Frances. "Music of Acoma, Isleta, Cochiti and Zuñi Pueblos." *Bulletin of the Bureau of American Ethnology,* Number 165. Washington: G.P.O., 1957. Chants on pages 12, 29, 45, 52, 77.

— *Music of Santo Domingo Pueblo, New Mexico.* Southwest Museum Papers, Number 12. Los Angeles: Southwest Museum, 1938. Chants on pages 40, 68.

Mathews, Washington. "Navajo Myths, Prayers and Songs." *University of California Papers in American Archaeology and Ethnology,* Vol. 5, No. 2. Berkeley: University of California, 1907. Chants on pages 43, 72, 79.

— "The Night Chants, A Navaho Ceremony." *Memoirs of the American Museum of Natural History,* Vol. VI. New York: American Museum of Natural History, 1902. Chants on pages 18, 20, 56, 62, 75, 80.

Mindeleff, Cosmos. "Navajo Houses." *17th Annual Report of the Bureau of American Ethnology* (1895-1896). Washington: G.P.O. Chants on pages 51, 58, 103.

Newcomb, Franc, and Reichards, Gladys. *Sandpaintings of the Navajo Shooting Chant.* New York: J.J. Augustin, Inc., 1937. Chant on page 96.

O'Bryan, Aileen. "The Dine: Origin Myths of the Navaho Indians." *Bulletin of the Bureau of American Ethnology,* Number 163. Washington: G.P.O., 1956. Chants on pages 11, 64, 84, 92.

Spinden, Herbert J. *Songs of the Tewa.* New York: Exposition of Indian Tribal Arts, 1933. Chants on pages 23, 39, 48, 55, 70, 82, 95, 99, 106.

Stevenson, James. "Ceremonial of Hasjelti Dailjis and Mythical Sand Painting of the Navajo Indians." *8th Annual Report of the Bureau of American Ethnology* (1886-1887). Washington: G.P.O. Chant on page 46.

Wheelwright, Mary, and Klah, Hosteen. *Navajo Creation Myth: The Story of the Emergence.* Santa Fe, New Mexico: Museum of Navajo Ceremonial Art, 1942. Chants on pages 36, 90.